Restless Spirit

Joyful by Design
Tallahassee

Restless Spirit
Ken Williams
Published by Joyful by Design 2019
Tallahassee, FL
First edition; First printing

Copyright © 2019 Ken Williams
All rights reserved. Do not share or forward this work, or reproduce any portion by any means, without written permission of the author. Fair use of quotes and key concepts must be appropriately cited.

www.joyfulbydesign.com
ISBN 978-0-9976590-9-2

I dedicate this book to my wife, Rene Williams. Thank you for caring enough to tear down the walls and discover the real person inside of me. Allowing me to delve into my past and deal with my broken heart. Giving me time to heal was instrumental in my search and desire to conquer a lifetime of struggles and addictions. Continuing your love and belief in me has been vital in the process of my healing. Your love has enabled us to create a spiritual journey for the both of us that to this day, we stand in awe of our Lord and Savior, Jesus Christ, without whom I would not be writing. I want to thank you, my dear, for accompanying me on this search, which at times has been very painful for us both. I only ask we both continue this journey the Lord has created for us. Most of all, I humbly and sincerely thank our Heavenly Father for guiding us on our journey.
Thank you, Lord - I praise your name.

Restless Spirit

Ken Williams

Tallahassee

Poems

Restless Spirit

Unspoken
Where
Epiphany
Abyss
Forever my Pain
Catharsis
A Higher Plane
Darkness
Goodbye My Lover
Forgiveness

Transcendental
Life Comes Full Circle
My Wife
Still Crazy
Ode to Brother Joe
Adrianne
The Griner's 3
Shrimp Tales
Papa Said
Love Has No Boundary
Bad Boys

Faith or Works
A Work in Progress
Why Me, Lord?
Chemistry
Discipline (Love)
The Power of the Word
Today I Became a Gardener
Cry (Charles Geiger 09.05.69)
Unknown Soldier
Danny Boy
Realization

Restless Spirit

Troublesome most of my life
The ongoing internal struggle and strife
With this condition, I cannot describe
For no one, would I subscribe
This feeling, stirring, craving
For more, different, new, I cried
Goes without saying, the things, I sighed
The very things I adore the most and yes
These things I have created, a restless mess
Now my God has brought me out of the abyss
Now I see the light and its conclusion, don't miss
For it was my search, God forgives me now
So it is my hope, all of you will somehow
Do the same and forgive me, for I knew not
The restless ecstasy, dark side, I caught
Finally, a glimpse of myself, I did not like
Thank you, God, for bringing me out into the light

✝ Restless Spirit ✝

Unspoken

Lest these words fall on deaf ears
What must be said will only bring tears
But must be said, before I am dead
These awful words, I always dread
I must leave you alone, not my desire
I cannot continue or I will expire
Loving you all my life must finally end
So, my love, these final words I must send
Do not feel sad, or begrudge my deed
Only for my protection, from your love, I secede
For I fear my life for you has only been a token
My love, today and evermore must remain unspoken

† Ken Williams †

Where

Ok Lord, I have a doozy for you this day
I am without a doubt, totally dismayed
Seems I got myself into quite a pickle
With this relationship so often been fickle
Longing for this woman all my life
All these years nothing to show but strife
Before you go accusing me
These things I'll say, you'll see
There has never been anything improper or wrong
It's just this woman
I can't rid myself – if only she were a song
I would play her again, again and again, so very much to enjoy
The music, the sounds, the touch, such joy
Alas, we are dealing with human emotion
Causing quite the commotion
Lord, I never meant for this to be hurtful or bad
Thought of never speaking with her again makes me sad
What am I to do?
What am I to do?
Forever I have cared for her, since we began, and it was new
Now all these years later, nothing has changed
I still long for her voice, her word, and have arranged
From time to time
To merely hear from her
It's a blessing, I know, Lord
I know with affairs of the heart we are a messin'
With pain and suffering though never meant to be
Such is our fate, unrequited love, I know you see
To love deeply in one direction makes us more loving in all others*
Tell me Lord, how can I turn away

✝ Restless Spirit ✝

From someone who touches my soul every day?
Even now when she is forever not here
This will not change, believe me, I'm sincere
If never I talk to or see her again
She will always be in my thoughts, my heart and soul
For love is unconditional, without agenda, so for me, this goal
To accept what I have, which is nothing
And as always in my heart I will play again and again
What could, should have been
Never let it become sin
Please let me know if all this is proper
If not, cease will I before becoming a problem, a whopper
This is all I have, or hope to have, asking nothing from her
Please tell me, O Lord, it's ok and allowed to occur
Your words I fear
Where do we go, where do we go from here?

✝ Ken Williams ✝

Epiphany

I knew this day was comin'
Just as the courts of the land would summon
What was I thinking?
Am I so cruel? Heartless?
In all my pain and suffering, did I create a mess?
Forgive me, my dear, I was only dreaming
Please, please do not think I was scheming
My thoughts of you are pure, but out of line
I should have realized, and surely missed my time
I have no right to pursue you in any way, shape, or form
What I have lived with all these years, I hope is not the norm
I could not, as always, help myself from dreaming and so
I will go back into my meaningless, little fantasy world of love
Conquering demons of the past, which fits as a glove
Never have I been able to erase you from my memory
I tried sex, alcohol, drugs…another story
I am weary of being the poor, hopeless romantic
With nothing to show, only the times I make me sick
My epiphany, as it were, is not as you probably think
God knows I would not do the normal way, just ask my shrink
Tis obvious to see my genuine care and yes, love for you
What have I been thinking all these years; we should start anew?
How ridiculous and insane, I have been derailed in advance
Journey to nowhere, without any hope or possibility of chance
That we could be together as I had dreamed
In my surreal, little carved out world, only a matter of time it seemed
Before we would be together, happy forever, no matter the price
Of all people, I should have realized the cost of rolling the dice

✝ Restless Spirit ✝

Removing all dignity and grace I have developed over the years
I should be thankful and in time I will
I know my journey in part was for you, because of you, still
It's tough for me to accept my fate and to you appeal
Unto your deepest most inner being, I one last time request
You realize who I am, what I am, and my very best
Has been and always will be yours to take
Please don't take, please don't take my heart, lest we both forsake
People who have loved both of us for all these years
I think I can't get over you
After all these years, what am I to do?
I will beg forgiveness from you and my Heavenly Father, you'll see
For being so foolish and hopelessly in love
With someone not meant to be
When I get to heaven and God permits a question or two
You know what I will ask…of course you do!
Why?

✝ Ken Williams ✝

Abyss

Dear Heavenly Father, we cry out to you today
We are heavy laden with trouble and hope that you may
Show us a sign, place in our hearts that we are on our way
Out of this misery, we pray you will deliver
For our wants are not for gold and silver
But we do have needs, needs of great demand
It is our debt and is our fault, let us not command
Lord – you know I need work – I am the man
I must work
I love work
Without work I cannot stand
We are thankful, we are humble and hope we are doing your will
Our troubles linger and weary we have become and yet still
We know you will provide – in this we truly believe
Lord, we humbly ask of you to relieve
This monster we have created and did conceive
Our prayer Lord is – show us a sign that we are on the right track
Thank you, Lord, for your promises and soon we hope to be back
We love you, oh Heavenly Father, and if it be thy will
Send us a sign and let us know, it's okay to be STILL

† Restless Spirit †

Forever my Pain

Today I am angry
I cannot speak
Anger overpowers and seems bleak
Anger over someone who's truth must never be known
I have come so far, purged my soul and have grown
Now the truth is out there, yet only I can see
Telling these truths is harmful and cannot be made public
Innocent people hurt, nothing can be gained
Here I am, the truth, am I insane?
I finally found and dealt with all the pain of my heart
But no one, not one, will know
I will start to figure what purpose there was for me to discover
Exorcising all this pain and suffering I used as cover
What am I to do now, what am I to do?
I only wanted to speak of (to) you
Dispelling the truth, my words, I will thrust
Into writing anonymously, I must
Alas, now…safe again
Forever my secret, forever my pain

† Ken Williams †

Catharsis

Writing now I am weary, weary as hell
Thinking of what I must tell
We've come so far – but have we really?
Of such things the world would say…silly
Why Lord? Why Lord? I cry out to you today?
You put us together, tear us apart and send us on our way
What cruelty, what pain, must be suffered yet again
Was this not your purpose, for us to regain
After all these years it's still there – I wonder why?
The reason no one can supply
I am tired of denying it and from now on I swear
To be truthful to myself, after all, is that not fair?
My feelings for you I cannot help
Should be stifled and placed on the shelf?
I have tried oh these many years to – yes…Alibi
Masking my feelings
Using many as a disguise
If I have one last shot to be honest perhaps it's true
I'm going to say the things that are long overdue
You are my one true love, it's always been said
Without you in his life he might as well be dead
Maybe this is too serious, too heavy to comprehend
For survival of my heart and soul I must defend
This part of my life simply must end.
I do not understand it and know deep down it is my fault
But for heaven's sake, haven't I been punished enough?
To all that disagree, I challenge you to rebuff
To live out your life knowing your biggest mistake

✝ Restless Spirit ✝

Has always been losing you
I am emotionally drained and must close now
Or forever be silent, figure out somehow
To tell you my love, how much I have truly cared
With what is left on my heart, to tell you I am scared
Where from here no one but you and I should know
I have loved you all my life
Unfortunately for me, you are another's wife
Goodbye my dear, I wish you well
With whatever you attempt to endeavor
For me, I wish so many years ago
To have been smarter, than so damn clever

† Ken Williams †

A Higher Plane

You say a small rendition
Allow me to say dear heart, in my condition
Word(s) from you I hold with the highest of regard
I have to be careful, my heart is at risk, so I must disregard
Any thoughts of you, I must savor and quickly put away
For if I continue on this ruinous path today
I will be yet lost again and forever be in pursuit
Of this totally impossible dream, I know 'tis moot
My hope is for you to understand of my heart the danger
As for me, I must confront and deal with my anger
Why again, and especially now, when my need is so great
Must I deal with the reality of it all, my heart aches
So now I humbly ask, for my heart's sake
May I say no to you?
Even though saying no may be worse to die
Don't feel bad, it's nothing you have done, it's matters of the heart
It happened long ago, August 27, 1963, the start
Perhaps you are correct it's meant for a higher plane
God help me find it before I go insane
I leave you now not to have you depressed
A real poet's words, not meant to impress
"I hold it true, whate'er befall;
I feel it, when I sorrow most;
'Tis better to have loved and lost
Than never to have loved at all."
Alfred Lord Tennyson

✝ Restless Spirit ✝

Darkness

On this cloudy, rainy, miserable day
I hear from a friend, in her voice, a ray
Sunshine I do desperately need to hear
I too am troubled, of what I do not know, with some fear
I pray for strength and patience, in her voice I hear God's reflection
Yet, I remain perplexed as to the circumstances and direction
What paths our lives are so inextricably on, seems parallel
This inevitable journey, why now? Do tell
I must know, if possible, why, all these events are linked
Please make it clear so I do not sink
Any further into darkness, some disturbing trait
I must not, will not, return, I've too long been straight
Made such progress
To revert back would be a shame and utterly useless
At time my life does appear to be exactly that...
It is demons, for all my life, I must combat
This evil of despair
Anger
Bitterness
I do fret
Please Got hold onto me and let me not forget
You are here for me, I know
Hear my cry
I am troubled not only for myself,
But also for my dear friend, I sigh
Hear my prayers O Lord, keep satan at bay
And please Got help me and perhaps my friend too,
Get through this day

† Ken Williams †

Goodbye My Lover

'Tis late at night, my thots, are sad
Me thinks not a way to be glad
My heart does ache, it is pain
Yet for me, much of this, gain
If never to have loved, we say
No hurt, no problem, but also no way
Thro life we will, we must
Love until we are dust
So, for me, dear heart
Sadness for me as we part
Enough already
Forget I did
Forget I not
Forget this time
My heart must stop

† Restless Spirit †

Forgiveness

In the Bible, Jesus says "forgive" seventy times seven
An infinite number in heaven
Please forgive your father and let him into your heart
No matter what he has or has not done let him start
Being the dad a little girl always needs
It is for both of you I plead
Don't miss one more day, for I see
A time when you will sit on his knee
And all will be forgiven as should
You have the rest of your lives and could
Enter into the most previous of relationships on this earth
After all is said and done – it will all be worth
For a father's love for his daughter is…well look at me
There is Nothing better, you'll see
My heart does ache for father and child
I have been where this dad is and feels beguiled
I know all can be forgiven, start anew
Let healing begin – you are both overdue

✝ Restless Spirit ✝

Transcendental

Now, alas, your knowledge of me, does transcend
You devour my writing and allow my soul to mend
Now I know my efforts are not in vain
You read them, then some measure of you I obtain
You must, therefore, know before I do, of what I write
You must know I do this, sincerely with all my might
I believe now, what starts only as pleasure
Is perhaps, the one earthly thing, I do most treasure
What a blessing you are to me
For you inspire me, like no other, you see
You do it for me, without asking return
I feel your passion, I sense your being, I feel your thot
So unselfish, so simple, so beautiful, as if I had bought
Something so special, but it's…your spirit, I have reserved
Of which, I seek, but do not deserve
Much said, believing, there was no more
But, sure as the eagles do soar
Inadvertently entering into this opening of your soul
Now ventured into, cannot look back, cannot control
My hope is for understanding, I defer
For I cannot, return to where we were

† Ken Williams †

Life Comes Full Circle

Life began oh so humbly one early morn
In June '47 a child was born.
So much was made of just having children – seems a pity
In this metropolis of Lake City
This boy they bore, 3rd in line of boys, his name was Kenny
All the others did not like, that he was so skinny
Not much expected from this kid who seemed dismayed
Cries of he's different than the rest, Ivan did say
To all the siblings who were laden with disgust
No meal, no food was a must.
All he wanted and requested was not to eat!
Was this a problem, to deal with or meet?
So Barb would allow him, everyday
To eat what he wanted, when he wanted,
Much to the sibling's dismay
Fifty years later Barb finds herself today
Stripped of her independence by the ravages of age (92 years)
Being forced by the nurses to eat – eat they rage
Guess who's there now to save the day?
Kenny says, Mom, eat what and when you want
We will have chocolate thank you, Barb did flaunt
Much to the chagrin of the nurses, was deafening their sighs
A moment so very pure, as they stared into each other's eyes
The devil could only cry
This very special Mom and son, a beautiful moment to share
No one would have predicted, the level of care
Thank you, Lord, for my Mom, I do pray
Life does indeed come full circle; it came this day!

✝ Restless Spirit ✝

My Wife

You have been with me from the start
When no one else could understand
Only you would know my heart
When others criticized, you were always there
Knowing things would work out
Only you would, only you could dare
Starting over armed only with our ability to care
No matter the situation, I think you knew
God was working in our lives
Evidenced as we grew
Growing together on our spiritual journey
It's clear for everyone to see
Our love is overwhelming, and everything it should be
I know you stuck with me for some time
More than you bargained for perhaps – maybe a crime
What a wonderful thing for both of us to have this ride
To where we are now, I can only sigh
Our lives were so wrong it makes me cry
A metamorphosis from a worthless existence
To following our Lord with love and balance
Now a meaningful life with purpose and promises from above
Filled with God's divine grace and love
We have come so far, and God is working out his plan
With God's help, will make a stand
Let's go forward together, let's enjoy God's mission for us
We will forever trust our Lord, until we are dust
God has molded us into something, for both of us he will use
Surely our old friends will laugh and only be amused
Our journey lay ahead, for we must do God's will
But today again, more than I want, we must be still

✝ Ken Williams ✝

Still Crazy

Since embarking on this journey of becoming a poet
My writings are raw, sad, perhaps I did not know it
I have spewed my heart's pain
It has always been uplifting and much gain
Challenged by thousands of my loyal subjects
To put a humorous slant on some of my next projects
Irony is I've been known more for my humor
As opposed to all the hurt I project, maybe a drunken stupor
Those who know me well
Never dreamed I had a serious thought, or possibly could
Write from my heart and soul with such gut-wrenching style
Funny, silly, stories they stretch a mile
Admitting to a few, just for credibility,
I expose, once again, my soul
Wow, I contemplate which one to choose, there are many told
I sold my beat up worthless moped, for a Mexican Burro,
Ok – a donkey
And God help me, rode her in the homecoming parade,
Egad, a honky!
Painted her hooves, purple and gold, of the mighty tigers paint
What the hell was I thinking, but was there a complaint?
No, because everyone knew I had something to prove.
Or for the more sinister, maybe I was working on my groove

✝ Restless Spirit ✝

Too many stories, too many tales, perhaps a book, I fear
Needed to tell all the stories and maybe you will hear
My best one, claim to fame, defining moment will always be
Night before leaving for the Air Force, and for "all" to see
Took my VW (Doodle Bug) into the Lake of Butler with all hope
It had been advertised and surely did believe, it would float
As the onlookers from the infamous loop
Did look on, it did not float
My pal Henry and I were gone!
The desire was for this to be funny, hoping it was for you,
Me, a little hazy
After all the years, I still hear echoing
In my ear…still crazy…still crazy.

✝ Ken Williams ✝

Ode to Brother Joe

I love my big brother Joe
And I have something to say
He was the best of the 3 brothers, let no one dismay
I described him at his funeral, and everyone did crow
We did not know he was like that, wish we did know
Why not…did you look? It was there for all to see
He was kind and humble and nothing like the generation me
He was a great guy with a delicious dry wit
He could easily make me laugh…the best story…I must admit
In the army the cook he said…patted out the hamburgers under his armpit
This left a lasting impression on me
So much so that I believe with no remorse
It's the reason my good friend Henry and I joined the Air Force
He will always be remembered by his own prophetic words:
I am a calm, cool steady guy – but who stole my lunch!!
God I love that – it was my big bro – he was no fluke
Yeah – that was my brother – Cool Hand Luke
Nothing bothered him, he was always the same
And with the women, oh yes, he did gain some fame
He was the best big brother a kid could have
He took up for me, allowed me to drive his cars, smoke, cuss, drink
It was really one of those (drive his car) I think
As only a big brother can be – he was my hero
But let no one else dare mess with any of the brothers three
We did love each other as much as can be
Now big brother, with many a tear in my eye
I miss you already and wish you had not died
As told at your funeral and swear this do I
I will not, cannot, say goodbye

† Restless Spirit †

Rather…I'll say…we'll see you later big brother
As always, I catch myself looking up to you like no other
Looking up indeed
See you in heaven – big brother

✝ Ken Williams ✝

Adrianne

To the lovely lady who I entrust my hair
Things to say today, to let you know I care
From the oh so sincere one who has all these years
Mispronounced your name, for now I fear
You will treat me equally and well I deserve
To shave my head, if you had the nerve
Alas, I stop trying to be a clown
Truly you are a blessing to me, with never a frown
We talk about our God, families, friends and such
Most of the time, it's really not much
We joke and laugh as stupid people who've come our way
Now I must tell you and tell you this day
I look forward to each and every time we meet
Cutting my hair, is not a big deal or feat
Seeing your smile and having a pleasant conversation is…
Important, and now I see you work in your station
Remind me what an idiot I must be
Mispronouncing your name, it's on your mirror for all to see
I implore you not to retaliate and shave off my hair
My fear is it will not grow back,
And a new customer you must snare
Forgive me for being silly, just wanted you to know I care!

† Restless Spirit †

The Griner's Three

What a surprise, never did I dream
The Griner's, forever my friends it seems
To grace me with their presence
In of all places my office, midstream
A delightful few moments, not enough for me
I had my best friend and family for all to see
What a blessing and I thank Jesus for sure
Made my day, with the daily burdens to endure
Forever thankful, this visit, a most worthy gift
Maybe now forgiveness for the saga of the shrimp
Harold promises never again to mention, lest I limp
This dreaded social fiasco, still hanging over my head
What friends you are to me and let it be read
Sincerely, I say this to you, and I do not jest
Your visit, from my heart, has me blessed

† Ken Williams †

Shrimp Tales

Once up a time there lived a young boy named Kenny
Unbelievable as it may seem now, he was so skinny
This lad raised by Ivan and Barb, of Lulu fame
He was so precocious, eager to learn
His good friend Harold Griner did discern
Kenny was in need of culture, refinement, it seemed
His pal Harold, invites him to his home and dinner, no less
Yes, the menu, the delicacy, shrimp, before you guess
At the Griner home, dinner was proper, mannerly I suppose
The story from here on out – is a matter of disagreement
And who knows
If Harold is telling the truth, or is it possible
This rube, this sod buster, this crazy boy,
Is telling the Gospel, I digress
I'll tell you the facts and let you decide
Who was telling the truth and please be on Kenny's side
The dinner, shrimp, was delicious, although a little crunchy
Even at the end, Kenny, remained munchy
After the meal and as the cultured family discussed world events
Harold asked, how did you like the shrimp?
Ok, said Kenny, and another question from my inquisitive friend
How many shrimp did you eat?
An insane question, how the heck would he know,
Leaping to his feet
Harold simply replied, count the tails, and the number it will deem
A not so simple request, for a country boy it seems
The number you ate, he replied, you do, surely have tails left?
At that moment, Kenny boy, realized what it means to be deft
For he was moving, thinking, ninety to nothing, to explain
He thought of faking a heart attack, or a seizure or just a feign

✝ Restless Spirit ✝

That he actually meant to eat the tails, you see
Harold would have no part of this lie, and forever on me
He would hold the most embarrassing moment in this boy's life
Over his head, particularly in the
Company of young women he would delight
Letting on about this boy,
Who did not know one end of the shrimp from the other
And boy, did he ever humiliate him,
Time and time again, like a brother
Don't feel bad for this little country boy, humiliated forever
After all these years, Harold is an artist, who does endeavor
To be accomplished, and he is, but perhaps he does not remember
His very first art (painting) was given to this boy,
In 1970, around September
It was not perfect, according to Harold, his own worst critic
To this boy, it was special, it's even now out of the attic
No amount of money, could buy this special first painting, no way,
For Kenny, is waiting, ever so patiently for Harold's success,
This day, at one of his most prestigious award dinners,
And the proper time for me
Kenny will show up with this "painting" for all the world to see
Harold, remember this painting,
For your party I do not want to crimp
Lest you forget, how many did you have of the shrimp?

† Ken Williams †

Papa Said

It's long been a source of natural contention
Wives for me, there was no retention
Puzzled me for some time
Although, being divorced and remarried seemed no crime
I never planned to be a punch line for all to hear
At times this conversation does make me tear
Some of the more cruel or harsh ones, it's said
He can't stay married, he'd rather be dead
Honk, if you've been married to Kenny, once made me proud
Now let me say, and please listen, I will say out loud
Running through many relationships, marriages was not my plan
I was hurting, and do apologize for all I have banned
During my journey, I never enjoyed leaving people behind
I felt gallant, somehow kind
Doing them a favor, leaving, I was in such pain
So much so, how could anyone have gained
I did not intend for this to be sad
Actually, it's to be funny, and about my Dad
Ivan, Papa, we called him, was such a wonderful man
He was country boy smart, a man of few words, please understand
When he spoke, we paid attention
At my parents 50th wedding anniversary, I must mention
I was already divorced, one marriage down and working on another
He asked of me, why isn't one woman enough, as I looked for cover
Leaning over to me, and in his very special way
Never have I forgotten his words of wisdom that day
I did not have an answer, finishing our father-son chat
Long overdue, Papa said
You're not going to have one these, are you?

✝ Restless Spirit ✝

Love has No Boundary

I have thought of this subject often, greater minds than me
Pondered this truth and now, for all to see
Wonder of the human, who can love with such fervor
Places restrictions, as if, love has a maximum, we all endeavor
To limit, restrict, *own* or selfishly guard....how insane
Love has no periphery, it cannot, it will not, lest it be vain
I dare say, this thing called love, I have finally found
Must be total, all encompassing, but mostly profound
Love conquers all, if you think not, you have not loved
Love is so wonderful, love is everything, and it comes from above
If this is not true, then this writer, has never drawn a breath
I believe love is everything, and upon my death
Let it be written, let it be said, this writer did love
God may have taken everything else, my beloved
But he gave me love and allowed me love, what's left to say?
I am thankful God, to you, for allowing love to come my way
Let it be said, let no one doubt, forever I have been smitten
Know this today, I loved, I was loved, let it be written
Love, truly has no boundary....

† Ken Williams †

Bad Boys

Always love the bad boys
You know, the ones that make the noise
They lead with their heart, do not alert
There is no other way to avert
For they are in such need, I sigh
It is for your love they do cry

✝ Restless Spirit ✝

Faith or Works

A subject, that has, as a Christian, always perplexed
Is it Faith, alone, as the legalist would have you believe?
Or is it works, by which we are saved, too complex?
James, brother of Jesus, knew the answer
A leader in the Jerusalem Church, he saw unchristian behavior
Christians who followed the letter of the law, but forgot
To love, to help, yes to love as would our Savior
They say they believe in God, but to look at them
You would not see any sign of love for their fellow man
Perhaps this is what disturbed me most as a young Christian
Faith yes, works no, but could quote scripture, and never did occur
This agape love, where was it, I could not stand
Talking the talk but not walking the walk, it did not fit
For Christians are supposed to be about love,
The number one command
We are to care for the needs of our fellow man, I submit
Is there any better way, than to emulate our Savior
Love thy lord, with all thy heart, mind, soul and strength
Thou shalt love thy neighbor as thyself, yes, our neighbor
A Christian has an inward drive to please God, such a labyrinth
We please God, by bringing God the glory
It comes from a heart of love given to us by a God of Love
A Christian sees a need and responds accordingly,
This should be the story
Faith and works are inseparable, it comes from above
You cannot have one without the other, it is said
Make no mistake, this is important
As the body without the spirit is dead, so too, faith without works is dead!

✝ Ken Williams ✝

A Work in Progress

So surreal this thing called age
The sound, the word, can cause rage
Why do we do this, why you say
The Bible states, it's an honor, do not be dismayed
For your elders (egad) are to be respected
And the Lord, thy God, to be revered
Leviticus 19:32, to my eye brings a tear
Sailing through life, did I until the age of forty, 4 - 0
Nothing bothered me, nothing could, I did crow
But since this time and no coincidence, I was reborn
I have been on this fateful journey and at times I feel worn
There have been many times lo, all these years
When I did backslide, and let satan foster my fears
God I truly love you, and thank you for my ride
Thankful you have rid me of my worst….my pride
God help me stay the course and be what you want me to be
For the first time ever, I have prayed, upon my knee
Praying, I have done before but not like this, you'll see
To take my life and make it (me) whatever your (not my) will
I know soon you will answer and yet still
I await your decision and I will render
To your desires for my life, I hereby surrender
Make me, mold me, whatever is your will
I will seek your presence in whatever I do, with all my might
All credit be to you, when I am successful in your sight
Thank you Lord for your patience with me and for taking so long
Discovering where you will have me go and belong
To do thy will and your purpose for my life I seek
It's scary Lord, it's scary, I am weak
Without you, I am nothing, but alas, I digress

✝ Restless Spirit ✝

Truer words, have never been spoken
I am, indeed, a work in progress
These words represent for me a humble badge of honor,
Although, you may find them redundant
Words that are mindful of a humble request, perhaps now urgent
My children, my wife
Will probably quote these words when I'm dead
Thank you Heavenly Father
Maybe someday my words will be read
Humbly I await your sign of what you would have me do
Lord, I am waiting on thy word, nothing new
Shield me with your armor, continue the Journey will I
This Glorious New Chapter, according to your will, until I die

† Ken Williams †

Why Me, Lord?

Father, indeed, you have a sense of humor
My friends are worried, there's even a rumor
Somethings happened to him, they say
We've heard, he does pray
What is wrong with him, what has he done
He must have done something and be on the run
We don't understand his behavior, his demeanor
There is a calmness about him, not easy to ignore
He is always speaking of Jesus, as if he knew him
Ah yes, Jesus, on my face a grin
Always I have pulled for the down and out
Ironic, now, I am on your team, I shout
It's the way you accomplish your tasks
For you, no matter who is behind the mask
You sent Gideon, a weak diminutive man
To destroy the most ferocious army in the land
Gideon did triumph over the Midian army, for all to see
Gideon, it's said, once asked the Lord…why me?
Saul, persecutor of Christians, surely God would not push
For a man like him, as he fell on his knees, at the burning bush
Saul, it's said, once asked the Lord…why me?
Now two warring nations decide to fight one on one
The Philistines chose Goliath, and my God chose a son
Youngest son of Jesse, a little shepherd boy,
Not even the most smart
Slays Goliath, becomes king, and a man after God's own heart
David it's said, once asked the Lord…why me?
Indeed, some very odd choices, my God does choose
Your ways are mysterious, nothing new
You take the weak, the least likely, the last one

✝ Restless Spirit ✝

The unwanted, the downtrodden, and always it's done
Through you, O Lord, I simply adore
I have wasted so much precious time against you Lord,
Allow me to make up for this crime
Lord, maybe you can use me
To do Your work, and surely, I am the most unlikely person to be
Chosen for any of your tasks, but listen and you will see
You do pick men like me, fallen, sinful, and weak
To do special things and peak
Your will, O Lord, what have you chosen for me?
I have none of the credentials required, it's just me
I love the way you do things, O Lord
You use the mightiest, the most powerful, of the sword
And sometimes, yes sometimes, it is very plain to see
To do your work, you pick sinners, you pick men like me
So now I must ask you Lord…why me?

✝ Ken Williams ✝

Chemistry

A periodic table of elements it's not
For most the subject is quite hot
Chemistry – Attraction
What say ye about all this nonsense
Do you not know it's all pretense?
Some say it's all about the pheromones
Perhaps it may be chemical – attraction
A man could be attracted to someone merely
Because of something not tangible, not really
Oh, but does it ever – doth say all – appeal
The mere thought of it does seem surreal
Let me tell you of this wonder
For me it has been real, as real as thunder
So real that after 45 years and counting
It's still there. Whatever it is
It's something that actually hurts inside
Not pain, you decide
It must inside you reside
So wonderful, it makes me cry
The most beautiful hurt, a hurt so fine
For me it has defined
My very existence has depended on this thing
For every day of my life since had a ring
A ring? How dare you boast of such dribble
Maybe it's not real after all, I dare quibble
Without it, we might as well be dead
Ah, but don't you say it, or upon your head I will dink
This thing called Chemistry – Attraction, it is nothing
It's nothing all right. It's only…everything

† Restless Spirit †

Discipline (Love)

Most of my life a word I found most distressing
Was not a fan, did not believe it was for me
Now after all these years I find it inseparable
From all I do, and it is all so necessary for my life
Take love for instance, God loves me not because
I am lovable but because it is God's nature to do so
I too am to love as He has loved me, love people that
Sometimes not wanting to…yet must exhibit love as He did for me
Neither natural love nor divine love will remain
Unless it is cultivated, love is spontaneous
But it has to be maintained
Oh yeah, by the word I used to hate, discipline

† Ken Williams †

The Power of the Word

I know in my heart there is great need
A most humble servant, I am, indeed
I do not know if I am a poet or not
But no matter, I cannot stop
What matters, doeth these words of mine
Maybe, just maybe, in time
Someone will read and be touched
Affirming the effort without a crutch
This hunger, this desire, this ache to give
Something meaningful, for all by which to live
Please know the power of the word for good
The power, the awesome power we all should
Go through each day armed with the word
To love, and know what it is to receive
The blessing of a good word, do not be deceived
My writing, who knows maybe in prose…
Or maybe, I cannot complete a sentence, who knows?
But, if by some of my words, a person is moved
To love more, give more, and their life improved
Then all is for the better and maybe I am sane
The mere sound of a good word, don't we all gain?
Our very existence depends on the word, we truly need
Sometimes it's just the planting of a seed
Release the power of the word, it can change a life
Give and give, this most precious of gifts, reveal it's might
Love deeply, love covers a multitude of sins
Impact lives, help set their destiny, now is the time to begin
I implore you to bestow on someone else, the power
This most incredible of deeds, may just be your finest hour
Mindful of the importance of the word always endeavor

† Restless Spirit †

Knowing the impact, after all it is…forever
Remember the power…of the word, less we regret
For if my words mean anything, perhaps worthy, never forget

† Ken Williams †

Today I Became a Gardener

Today, heartbroken, while toiling in my yard
An elephant ear tree, I did not like, struck me very hard
'Twas the intricacies and absolute wonder of it all
That was spun and woven perfectly that made me feel so small
I read today…God was going to reveal himself to me
And brother did he ever, so wonderfully to see
What a miracle it is to see God's beauty
And purpose for every living thing
And what a small part God has for me, but to praise Him,
Praise Him, I sing
That His perfect beauty of this work (elephant ear tree)
Was always there
But I could not see because of the needless burdens that I bear
No more my God – you have my attention –
What beauty there is for me
Thank you for opening my eyes to the lovely,
Beautiful elephant ear tree!
Help me Lord, be a good steward
And in all living things see the beauty
I pledge now to be more aware, as such will be my duty
Not to allow my heart to ever again be hardened
And if ever I do, will simply go walk in the garden.
Thank you, Lord.

† Restless Spirit †

Cry (Charles Geiger 09.05.69)

I hear you buddy, I hear you loud and clear
Your life was taken, life we all hold so dear
The news, the tragedy we all wondered why
Friends, all of us wondered why you had to die
Vietnam, the sixties, it was such a turbulent time
Doing your patriotic duty certainly no crime
Remembering the day, Harold sent me the news
Killed on the battlefield, our friend Charlie we lose
This fateful day, upon hearing of your demise
(Harold) drove straight down to the lake, could only cry
We miss you Chuck, image you today
What you would do and what you would say
Realizing nothing would have changed you
And nothing should
You were such a cool guy, perhaps for the day, too cool
And if you were alive today you would rule
We talk about you often, never out of our thoughts and prayers
Funny things remembered about you, displaying your wares
A corvette, motorcycle, and your Elvis-like lip
Kicks man, kicks you were so very hip
We laugh thinking how fun it was, with you to hang around
What a trip you were – all of us a bunch of clowns
Miss you, love you man and for as long as we all shall live
Always pondering why…
You had so very much to give

✝ Ken Williams ✝

Unknown Soldier

At the Charlotte, NC airport, I saw something I could not ignore
Witnessed a young soldier, leaving for war
His young wife, and baby, sobbing uncontrollably
He was being strong and courageous, but I could see
His heart breaking, for he did not want everyone to perceive
That maybe he was afraid of what lies ahead, his task
Just please allow, for today, him to wear this mask
Hiding his fears of the unknown and for his wife
He did not want her thinking this may end his life
Perhaps for this moment allow us to lean on each other
She will need this time, without me, she must be a good mother
He was ready and on a mission he signed on for
He would do his duty, serve his country, and not ask for more
Than to be safe, perform as he should and return undeterred
It is for his family, his honor, he does serve
My heart breaking, as I followed him
I quickly entered the airplane restroom to sob
Once upon a time, this was me, and I too thought it my job
But I digress, and I don't mean to make this about me
It's just my heart was breaking, for this young man, you see
He is going off, thousands of miles away, to risk his life
Now, for the moment, he can only think of his child and wife
I wanted to talk with him so bad
I didn't and it makes me sad
What I wanted to say, I will pray for God
To keep you safe from harm
I wanted to say, I will pray for you every day, angels will swarm
I wanted to, I wanted to, but with all my might
I just couldn't find the word that was right

✝ Restless Spirit ✝

Now as I close this, I find myself praying, for this young man
That God would speak to his heart and allow me if ever again
I see this young solider, or other ones too, allow me to say
What is in my heart, and don't let me put off another day
God in heaven loves you, my prayers go with you,
Be safe and secure
And thank you, I sincerely mean this, thank you, for what you do!

✝ Ken Williams ✝

Danny Boy

Danny Bennett today was laid to rest
Stealth was his style
From all who knew him best
How little we knew but perhaps his smile
All the mischievous times what a mess
His nickname was Broke-it
Understood only by his teammates
(I believe it was Ben net no…I broke it…)
Once in the heat of a football battle as a snap he dialed
Look! At that cheerleader! As only he could say
Another football perfect snap in the books
Danny was the Best Long Snapper in high school football
His talent was immense, snaps a work of art, truly beautiful
Administering a paddling one day to all the football players
For skipping school, Danny put a pencil in his mouth
Stepped up and said I will be first – Classic Danny
Most of all I will remember Danny as quiet and soft spoken
An introvert, when he did speak, we all listened
At our (1965) practice reunion (45) when asked to speak
He said so eloquently and perhaps speaking for all of us
"I have nothing to say."
Danny was in the Coast Guard, so I will close with this quote
"The Blue Book says we've got to go out and it doesn't say a damn thing about having to come back."
Sounds like the Danny I knew

✝ Restless Spirit ✝

Realization

All my life in pursuit of many women, of course younger
Now after all these years let no one put asunder
Carousing and chasing the elusive Butterfly
Of these things I have begun to cry
Looking back now I must band
Perhaps this is progress, understand?
For all my life with this endeavor has me battered
Now I realize, who it was…never really mattered.

Ken Williams, Decatur, AL
Married; Three children; Two grandchildren
Grew up humbly (polite word for poor) in Union County, FL
(Lulu & Lake Butler)

I originally starting writing over the years as a form of therapy. There were words and thoughts I needed to express; I had to write. My writing is honest, raw and emotional. I'm not certain these should be considered poems, but that form represents an honest interpretation on who I am and hope to be.

Please know some of my writing is what I consider "dark". I have always enjoyed sad songs not because they are depressing but because they touch my soul; my poetry is the closest I come to writing a sad song.

A quote from John Bradshaw: Evil is a source of moral intelligence in the sense that we need to learn from our shadow, from our dark side, in order to be good.

So, don't be alarmed about my dark side, it is something I have dealt with and continue to do so on my journey.

Finally, I love and have been inspired by Shakespeare's Sonnets, in particular number 81. I've included it here, dedicated to Connie Rivers Anderson.

> Or I shall live your epitaph to make,
> Or you survive when I in earth am rotten,
> From hence your memory death cannot take,
> Although in me each part will be forgotten.
> Your name from hence immortal life shall have,
> Though I, once gone, to all the world must die:
> The earth can yield me but a common grave,
> When you entombed in men's eyes shall lie.
> Your monument shall be my gentle verse,
> Which eyes not yet created shall o'er-read;
> And tongues to be your being shall rehearse,
> When all the breathers of this world are dead;
> >   You still shall live, such virtue hath my pen,
> >   Where breath most breathes, even in the mouths of men.

Ken Williams has used writing as a medium to capture memories for his family and friends for more than forty years. He lives and writes in Alabama.